Basic Supplies Polymer Clay • Pasta Machine

Tools

Acrylic brayer
Clay blade
Shaping tools
Sandpaper
Brushes

Basic Tools and Supplies

Pasta Machine – is essential to claywork. It makes preparation of the clay and thin layers possible.

Polymer Clay Blade – is an extremely thin long blade. You need a flexible one for curves, a rigid one for straight cuts and slicing.

Roller – acrylic brayer or roller. Clear so you can see through it and detect any contamination on it.

Tools – craft knives, embossing tool, needle tool, bone folder, carving tools, shaping tools – any 'clay' tools that will help to manipulate shapes.

Set of mandrels or tubes – for making shapes, holes, and for smoothing.

Cutters, punches, templates – for making shapes.

Work surface – tile, acrylic, glass, marble, or other nonporous surface.

Oven – usually a convection or toaster oven that has been 'designated' for clay use. This is because the material (plasticizer) that keeps the clay soft burns off in the curing process and should not be mixed with food use. Use the oven in a well ventilated area.

Oven thermometer – This is the most overlooked but essential tool. Even a slight dip in temperature can result in a loss of strength in the finished piece. Cooking at too low of temperature can cause crumbling and cooking at too high can cause burning. Keep the temperature accurate according to the manufacturer's suggestions. It is also recommended to line several tiles on the oven racks to help regulate consistent heat. Use tin foil tented over the work to avoid scorching when a small oven is in use. Many toaster ovens 'surge' and make the clay items vulnerable to scorching.

Matte cardstock paper – is used to keep the shine off of clay when baking.

400 & 600 grit wet sandpaper – for sanding and smoothing finished pieces.

Buffer – for polishing sanded work. Clay can be drilled, carved, sanded and buffed after baking.

Deli wrap or wax paper – for storing canes. Some wraps will disintegrate over time, so choose a wrap that does not react to the clay. I recommend a soft plastic bead organizer. Never store clay in hard acrylic or expose clay to hard plastic (such as a computer).

Most challenging of all, the beautiful face cane can transcend beyond a cartoon rendering to evoke a delicate or engaging portrait.

Cane sets can build on related patterns and colors to create a unified theme. Here, the background is simulated ivory, in actuality, a cane.

Collected samples of cane work can continue to inspire throughout generations. These are examples of both new and old millefiori glass beads.

A cane can be an intriguing design principle, creating pattern, rhythm and movement in a composition.

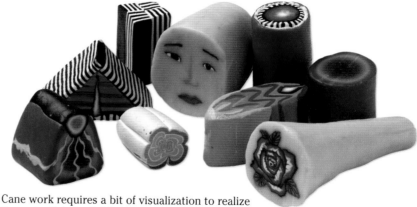

Cane work requires a bit of visualization to realize the potential of a finished piece of work originated from a group of canes.

Color

Color is everything. – No doubt about it, color will carry the piece. Basic rules in color apply, but each brand will have a specific color palette, that varies due to the saturation of the pigments in the clay color. There is no better way than to just 'try it! Here are my suggestions for color. Please note that these are my personal tips – not rules.

Always mix your color. With the exception of Black, White, translucent or pearl, any color will be enhanced with even a slight 'edge'. This personalizes your palette and sophisticates your work. Using color 'straight from the package' is recognizable and the sign of an underdeveloped work.

Mix a small portion to see 'what you get' – rather than mixing lots of clay and being disappointed.

Varying the value (light to dark) is more important than varying the hue (the actual color). The value is what creates dimension, vibrancy and depth.

Try to add even the smallest bit of Black or White into your design. This brings the full range of value (high and low) into a piece, and refines dimension. I believe Black and White serve as 'referees' to a color combination that may otherwise fight for attention.

Know your style – bright or subtle, you work best as YOU. Your distinct color choices are as identifiable as any theme.

Throw a CURVE. There is nothing safe about being an artist. Get out of the box once in a while. Life and color are full of surprises. Don't be skeptical until you've seen the completed results.

Color likes company. Like relationships, color 'pairs' well. The true beauty of a color is when it is in the company of another color.

Be satisfied with simple. Design is a refined taste. There's always tomorrow for complication.

Lust for the next project. Love what you are doing so much you can't wait to do it again.

These blended strips can be used as reference or added to an entire sheet of translucent, white or pearl clay to extend and color new sheets.

Skinner Blend

One aspect of color and caning that forever changed the sophistication of polymer clay was the introduction of color blends. Named after Judith Skinner, the "Skinner Blend" is a quick and easy method for blending and transitioning one color smoothly into another without harsh defining lines. Many textbook examples begin with an overlapping of two elongated right triangles that uniformly and proportionately blend two colors, but – hey! then there's real life. My versions of the blend are a rag – tag heap of color that magically and controllably melts into a sonnet of tints and shades (adding White is a tint and adding Black is a shade).

 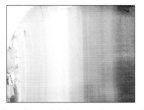 

Directions for random blending: Make any heaps of clay into flat sheets by rolling into a flat pancake shape and then pass through the pasta machine.

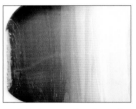 

• Or if using solid sheets of color, align one next to each other in a sequence so the colors tilt. This is usually done in sheets where the colors are arranged at angles (slight or dramatic) next to each other. All of the sheets should be the same thickness, so the blend can be estimated proportionally. Dramatic angles will produce gradual blends and vertical angles will produce sharp blends.
• The colors will blend proportionally as aligned along a vertical axis.

Directions for Measured Folding: Make two triangles that meet along a middle diagonal. Fold the aligned sheet in half, from top to bottom keeping the same color on the right (or left) each time you fold. WARNING: Mixing up the fold will blend all the clay into one color. Hint: Once the clay is flattened, move the rollers to a smaller setting to blend faster.

- Pass the fold through the pasta machine over and over (folding and passing) until it produces a smooth blend.
- Note: The sheet will creep (horizontally) to the sides of the pasta machine.
- If you don't like a blend - you can add another color to it to change the hue.

Suggestions for Blends

Rules of saturation apply – for example, red will overpower almost all the colors in blending, so use accordingly (sparingly).

Even the smallest dab of color will effect white or translucent. To make pastel anything, you need a lot of white (or pearl).

White can be pasty- but can really 'pop' highlights.

Pearl colors add the mica sheen to clay and can add a rich luster, although Metallic or Mica clays (pearls) will shift the reflection, and may create unwanted 'lines' - not recommended for faces. Also pearls will 'darken' a cane when cut into a cross section. The illustrious reflections will not show!

Translucent canes will create 'see-through' layering. Caution not to place over dark colors. Translucent to opaque blends can be really cool!

Bordering a blend in Black can create a Black 'wrap' when the sheet is rolled into a cane.

Vary the value. Color blends of the same value have no contrast and are dull.

I appreciate working from light to dark, or in a three color blend, placing the lightest in the middle.

Don't skimp on quantities. A good blend is always used up.

To 'extend' a color, or make a larger quantity, place a full sheet of translucent over the blend.

To lighten an entire blend, place a clay sheet of white or pearl over the blend.

Use sections of a blended sheet for different projects.

Blends will always creep to the width of the pasta machine.

Black is not the enemy! Adding Black to a blend can make gorgeous shades (especially gold)

Keep color sample strips to reference as great blends!

Store scrap in piles of 'like hue' so you can make blends at a later time. This recycles scraps! Not all blends need to be stored as sheets – only when they are run through the pasta machine.

Use blends as backgrounds to decorated beads, switch plates, bracelets, etc.

Color does not have to be glaring to be effective. Cynthia Toops elegantly combines desaturated color and bold form to create wonderfully clean and organized design. The finished quality of the work adds value to the artistry.

Exquisite wire work by Lisa Barth frames a single Kaleidoscope bead. The designer has captured the color from the bead to strengthen the overall presentation.

Playful color is most effective when it includes high and low color values. This is illustrated in the use of Black and White in each of these bicone beads by Barbara McGuire.

Shaded or blended color makes an impact in both canes and backgrounds. Large areas of space create dimension with subtle shading in these beads by Barbara McGuire.

 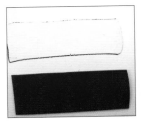

Basic Spiral

The spiral can be easily described as a jelly roll. It is basically just that – a roll of layers.

These layers and colors and thicknesses can be infinitely variable and create dramatic effects, but even a plain old jelly roll is an invaluable design element.

Black & White Spiral: Roll two sheets of clay, same size. In this example the Black sheet is slightly thinner than the White sheet. Stack sheets together. Taper one edge with a brayer. Carefully begin to roll sheets (like rolling a carpet) at the tapered edge. Continue until the roll is completed.

Red, Black and White: Spiral: Roll a thick sheet of Red clay, and very thin sheets of Black and White. Trim sheets so they are about the same size. Stack the Black and White together and run together through the pasta machine. When rolled, these thin sheets will look like a thin pen line.

Place the Black and White sheet, Black side down and position the Red sheet on top. Proceed to roll so the Black sheet is on the outside of the roll.

Three Color Spiral: It is as important to vary the value in a design as it is to vary color. Choose colors by light or dark to create dimension.
• Stack the three sheets of color from dark to light. Trim and taper the stack for rolling.
• Roll the stack together. The seam will create a 'registration mark' for future assembling. To reduce the cane, place both fingers in the middle of the cane and roll with even pressure towards the outer edges. I prefer to reduce canes in gradual sizes, as this leaves more design options open.

 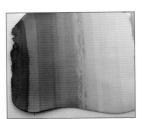 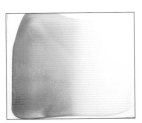

Shaded Spiral with Black Outline: Create a blend that graduates from dark to light. Cut a strip section of the blended sheet to use for a spiral cane. Note: Every time you make a blend, you can divide the sheet and use it for different purposes, as this helps to create 'sets' of canes with like colors.

• Place the strip on a thin sheet of Black. Trim to equal size. Taper the light end.
• Roll the strip into a 'jelly roll'. Note: If the Black clay begins to split, instead of rolling flat, pick the clay up and coax the sheet around the core without splitting. When rolled, these thin sheets will look like a thin pen line.

Spirals

The spiral – as infinite as time.

I used to think if I made a spiral, I was 'copying' someone (most likely someone famous), and I would probably be outcast forever as someone who never had an original idea. It was only years later that I began to look at the spiral as a tool - a timeless, fascinating tool for original interpretation.

There are more ways to make a spiral than imaginable and it is just one of those fundamental designs that has been around forever and nobody owns. Pick it up and run with it. You will be surprised at its magic!

Spiral Kaleido Quilt

Sometimes you can 'overdo it' with canes and it just looks busy. Then you can take the cane one step further to modify its original intention. By cutting and reassembling this square spiral, make a cane resembling a quilt pattern. The quilt pattern can also be wrapped with layers to define and outline the pattern.

Barbara McGuire set tiny crystals in rows of rainbow spirals to make a charming barrette.

• Stack colored sheets and shaded sheets and trim to equal size. The illustration shows Black, Red, White and a Green shaded sheet.
• Taper the edge and roll the stack carefully. Since the stack is thick, it is more prone to splitting.
• Complete the roll.

• Pinch the cane into a square form, beginning with the edge placed in one corner.
• Reduce the cane by rolling the brayer on the edges. Flip, rotate and invert the cane clockwise and counterclockwise as you roll on each edge. It is important to distribute the pressure in all the directions, as the cane will become lopsided if it is only rolled clockwise.
• When the roll is reduced to approximately 1" slice off the ends until the complete cane design is revealed. The ends appear distorted, but the design will eventually emerge. It is important for building complicated canes that each component be whole, free of distortion.
• Cut the cane into 2 equal parts, about 1½" long. Note: it is easier to work with short wide pieces rather than long thin ones. Slice through each cane section diagonally. Reassemble the cane slices with the corner edge to the inside. Trim the cane evenly, cutting off the 'lip' of the tail to straighten the cane (the little piece that doesn't belong in the pattern sequence).

Tapered Spiral

MATERIALS:
Basic tools
Thick Sheet (thickest setting) of skinner blended colors (3 or more), blended from dark to light
Thin sheet of Black, thin sheet of White

INSTRUCTIONS:
Cut two 2" wide strips from a sheet of blended color. Stack the sheets together so they are about ³⁄₁₆" thick. (Stack more strips if needed.)

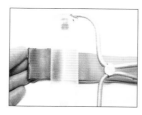 

• Taper the stacked sheets with your roller by pushing one of the ends (in this case – the darker end, gradually into the roller.
• Elongate the rest of the strip by pulling and rolling with the brayer to make the stack thinner on the lighter end. The end of the strip should taper to a very thin edge.

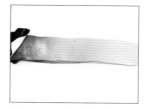 

• Stack the Black and White sheets together and place the colored strip on top of the White sheet. Trim. Taper the thin edge to include the Black and White sheets.
• Roll the spiral up starting at the thin edge. Do not push the tail of the spiral into the cane, if you want the cane round; cut the tail to the curve of the cane.

Tips for Spirals

Vary the value in your blend, or when adding two colors together. That means, make one light and one dark. Even complementary colors that would normally send your eyes spinning, will behave if one is tinted (adding White) and the other is shaded (adding Black)

Try using White as an outline color.

Try using a very, very thin Black, along side of White, as the defining outline.

Wrap your spirals with the Black on the outside so they won't get dirty.

Reduce the same cane to different sizes; even tiny spirals catch the eye.

Taper the spiral simulating a nautilus. The spiral becomes more alluring.

Blend the colored sheets from light to dark, to create depth and movement.

Be sure the clay is well conditioned. A thin sheet of stiff clay will split or separate, leaving gaps.

Max Spiral

Covering large areas with a continuous flowing spiral can be effective as a design element, or as a background. These large flat canes are meant to be made 'as is' and not necessarily reduced.

The cane is sliced across, not down in cutting cross sections for use.

Tips for Max Spirals

MATERIALS:
Basic tools
2 Blended sheets of clay color ranging from dark to light

1. Varying values is as important as varying the color, if not more so. In this cane, the value (light to dark) creates the contrast not the color.

2. Not all spirals need to be Black and White. Try shades (adding Black) or tints (adding White) to the same color to make interesting spirals.

3. Vary size of rolled sheets to make 'different' spirals.

Even the crude and rough 'ends' of the max spiral cane add flavor to this appliquéd painting by Barbara McGuire.

   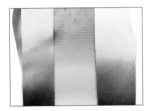 

• Make a vivid blend by adding White on one end to make the brightness 'pop'.
• The blend illustrated has a variety of brilliant colors that will be softened in the blending.
• If the colors are too 'stripy' tilt the sheet as you fold it and run it again through the pasta machine several times. Have faith!
• The second blend can be any colors, note that the colors in the stripe will be alternated between high and low value, so when choosing the mating sheet, look for contrast.
• Stack the two sheets together, one on top of the other, placing opposite values at each side.

• Slice into 4 sections and stack on top of each other, creating alternate color stripes.
• Cut this cane in half lengthwise with the intention of doubling the height of the stripes. You will get a thin but high stack of stripes. You have to accomplish this while the cane is on its side.
• The next step is to reduce one end of the cane by pinching, pulling or rolling together with a brayer. Leave the other end as wide as possible.
• Cut the pinched scrap off and roll the tapered end into a spiral. It helps to roll the spiral flush with the work surface.
• The finished spiral should be a tight roll of color, shifting values along the diminishing spiral.
The spiral shown is about 1" high. It is intended to be utilized in its actual size and should be sliced across the design of the cane.

The Bull's Eye

The bull's eye, along with the spiral and stripe, create a foundation for most of the shapes in cane building. Good habits and color concepts carry through to all canes, making these simple projects fundamental in building skills.

The basic design appeal in a circle is not to be underestimated, it is innate and core in its value.

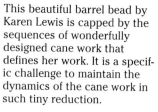

This beautiful barrel bead by Karen Lewis is capped by the sequences of wonderfully designed cane work that defines her work. It is a specific challenge to maintain the dynamics of the cane work in such tiny reduction.

The Blended Eye

Although a solid color is just fine, once you have experienced a blend, it's hard to resist using it in all your canes.

Blended color sophisticates a simple wrapped cane and actually make 'rings 'of color easier to build. Blends, especially with a light core, add dimension to the circle, making them 'pop' out.

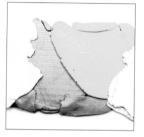

- Mix and blend colors as desired.
- Roll the sheet to the thickest setting and slice a section of the sheet across all the colors.

- Place the sheet into the pasta machine, beginning on one colored end and run the sheet through on the thinnest possible setting. NOTE: there is a point on some machines, where the setting is so thin it simply shreds the clay.
- These directions call for the thinnest setting you can handle without shredding the clay. You will get a very thin and long sheet. This may be hard to handle, so be prepared by having a surface to place the sheet onto.

- Beginning at one end, roll the sheet. The colors will gradually change as they wrap around the roll. Stretching the clay to a thin sheet is what makes the gradual change in color.

continued on page 10...

A small brilliant dot accents this wonderfully festive work by Donna Kato.

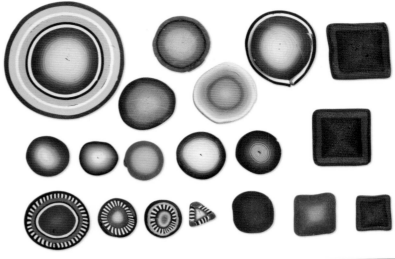

Simple slices from a bull's eye cane create a wonderful single bead in this graphic cane and glass necklace by Barbara McGuire.

Wrapped Bull's Eye

- Choose any solid color rolled into a cylinder, or create a blended roll.
- Make a sheet of White and a very thin sheet of Black. Layer the two sheets and trim to fit the length of the roll.
- Wrap the colored cylinder and with the prepared sheet, White side to the cylinder. As the wrapped sheet begins to overlap, pull it back gently and you will see a slight score line indicating where the wrap should be cut. Try to trim the sheet to fit exactly, or just short of exact. The clay will move to ease into place. Roll the cane to smooth the seam before continuing.
- Wrap with as many layers of color as desired. If you vary the thicknesses of the wrap, the cane will be more interesting.

Striped Bull's Eye

Choose any solid color rolled into a cylinder, or create a blended roll. Working in smaller sections, you will need a cylinder the length of the striped stack that wraps around it.

- Prepare a stack of alternating Black and White sheets. The layers will form a striped cane. Slice across the layers (similar to sliced bread) to create even slabs of stripe. The thicker the slice, the thicker the 'dashes' that will appear in the final cane. You will need several sliced slabs depending on the diameter of the cylinder.
- Place the striped slab on the cylinder so the stripes run lengthwise along the cylinder. Join several slabs to completely encircle the cylinder. You may have to cut the last slab to size, keeping the Black and White portions in sequence.
- Prepare a sheet of a contrasting color and wrap the cane, joining the sheet exactly at the seam.
- Wrap a final layer of Black clay. The purpose of this last layer is to outline the cane. If the stripes were not outlined, when the cane was pressed into a surface, the stripes (or dashes) could appear distorted.

Stripes

Stripes are about as simple, classic and variable as spirals and dots – and just as effective. They are perfect for borders and trims, and create rhythm in a cane design.

The long thin lines also create movement, another essential principle of design.

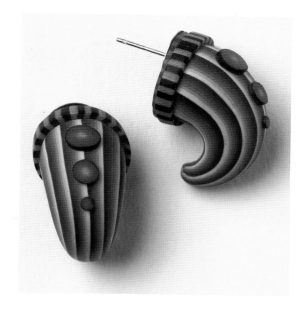

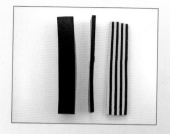 

Tips for Creating Stripes

A striped cane is literally a stack of alternating sheets of color. However, the more care to make the sheets even and trimmed, the better looking your stripes will be. Very thin striped can make you dizzy, so be careful not to reduce the layers too much.

Simulated ivory (a technique developed by Tory Hughes) is a stack of very thin layers of bone and translucent clay. Bone is made by mixing equal parts White and ecru clay. The layers in the stack are thinner to begin with so reduction is easier. How thin the stripes should be is a guess (a personal choice) and the cane will expand as it is used in a surface.

• Measuring sheets helps to make the most of a stack. I like using a centering ruler. Measuring also helps when you cut the cane into equal lengths. Be sure to trim your ends so the design runs through the whole length of the cane.

• Think assembly through! Stripes can get the better of you if they are just slapped together – look at the sequences so each rotation has the same color to the outside.

Pinwheels
Arrange 4 striped squares in a pinwheel configuration to create a new look.

• Save scraps of stripes and do not 'pile' them. They make appliqués.
• Wrap stripes the same as you would wrap cylinders, with layers of varying color and thicknesses.
Reduce stripes by rolling with a brayer, flipping, turning and rotating the cane, clockwise and counterclockwise until it is the desired length. Be careful to exert even pressure or the cane will be crooked and the design slanted.

Donna Kato used the simple stipe and dot to create movement in this incredibly graphic style of earring.

Bargello

When working with polymer clay, it's helpful to transfer information or the experience of working with another media to the clay. This is obvious in the sense that techniques used to make Millefiori glass (canes!) were translated into clay, but other media may not be so obvious.

Fiber artistry is a good source of inspiration for canes – think of quilts. The technique of bargello is actually a needle working technique, where the stitches are moved up and down on the canvas or cloth to create a pattern.

Likewise, we can arrange strips of color in sequences that will create patterns in a striped cane.

MATERIALS:
Basic Tools
Sheet of blended clay, at least four colors.
• It's possible to create a blend, without making sheets but by simply joining progressive colors. Add pearl to the whole mix (to extend and add mica to the volume of clay) and White (on one end) to bring up the value on one end.

Bargello, continued on page 12...

Bargello, continued from page 11...

• Pancake or slice the log before running it through the pasta machine, so you don't damage your rollers. The first pass through the machine will spread the colors.

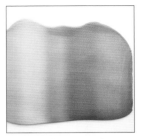 

• It's ok if the blends are more like stripes, and not a gradual blend.
• Cut the sheet into 5 even strips; almost separating the colors. Arrange the strips of color overlapping each section at the middle of the sections. Roll with brayer to even the sheet and run though the pasta machine to make the sheet flat again.

• Cut the sheet into sections again, this time <u>across</u> all the colors. Stack the sections, one on top of the other.
• Generally this will make a short stack, and you will need to cut this cane lengthwise in half, and double the amount of stripes.
To use the cane, you will slice across the stripes and use all or portions of the design.

Stripes are an effective border in these delightful earrings by Pier Volkous.

Chevron

The chevron is like a puzzle to me. I have to flip the sections several times before I actually get the pattern I want. And I always end up with too little of a cane.

For this reason, if you like chevrons, make a lot of canes. In this example, I made my cane into a feather.

• Prepare a shaded stack (as shown in Pyramid example) and slice diagonally into sections. The diagonals should be parallel. This cane calls for 4 sections.
• Flip the sections to alternate directions, aligning the stripes evenly. NOTE: It is important that you match the stripes as you place the cane sections next to each other. Begin as the canes touch and continue to align the cane exactly before you press it together. Move the cane around and pick it up so you can work with it. It doesn't need to stay on the work surface. In the illustration, I flipped it so the light color was at the top. NOTE: The color is not consistent in the stripe because of using a blended sheet. If you desire a perfect color match in the arrows – use solid sheets of color rather than a blend.

• My chevron wasn't looking very exact, so I made it into a feather. For descriptive purposes, I will call the points arrows. Pull the outer sides on the light end to envelope over the center 'arrows'. On the other end, (the base of the arrow), use a tube or rod to create a circle hollow. Fill this hollow with a teardrop cane (a cylinder flattened into a teardrop as shown in the previous project).
• To accentuate the light colors, and add more dimension to the cane, wrap another sheet of clay, a light color, over the top of the feather. This sheet only needs to extend halfway down the side of the cane.

Form the cane with your fingers into a desired shape and reduce slightly. This cane would most likely be used in appliqué.
TIP: Using tools to create hollows is a definite advantage. Whenever you place two portions of clay together, you will have a positive and a negative shape. These must match, or the two shapes (or one of them) will distort.

This is a collection of early beads by Barbara McGuire and can be reflected upon to realize that each cane gets better as you develop your style.

Repeated pattern creates a balanced symmetry in the borders of these cane slices by Barbara McGuire.

Colored stripes play a dynamic role in the pattern of this cane design by Lynne Ann Schwarzenberg.

Pyramid

The influence for this Striped Pyramid cane came from two respected peers of mine, Karen Lewis and Donna Kato. Both of these great artists employ a large amount of cane work in their art, which is a tribute to classic and timeless design.

Although design can be basic and generic, it is as interpretive the way the cane is applied that makes a distinguished piece.

• Roll a blended sheet with color values ranging from dark to light. The sheet should be set on the thickest setting. Section the sheet into strips, separating the values. In this example, I discarded the last strip because the value was so dark. Stack the strips in graduated value order with the lightest color on the bottom.
• Once the strips are stacked, turn the cane to its side. The cane will be about 1" high and be easy to work with. Cut through the cane at angles, making at least one triangle. The remaining cane was cut at angles to produce a chevron design. (shown in next project)
• Cut the triangle in half, or use the two ends shown to make a triangle shape. You will be placing a dividing shape in the middle of the triangle. Roll a shaded bull's eye of high contrast. The example here illustrates black and white. Cut a portion of the roll the height of the triangle and flatten the cylinder lengthwise to make an elongated teardrop. Place this teardrop in the middle of the triangle.

• Prepare a striped stack of alternating sheets of Black and White, and measure the stack the length of the triangle.
• Divide the striped stack into slabs (by slicing evenly) and place each slab on the sides of the triangle.
• Extend the corners to completely surround the triangle with a striped border.

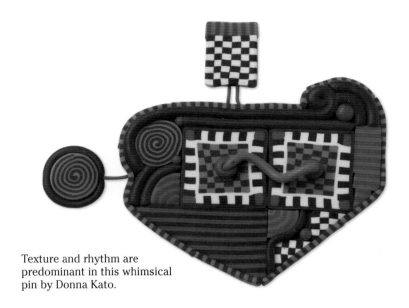

Texture and rhythm are predominant in this whimsical pin by Donna Kato.

Checkerboard Cane

The checkerboard is a familiar pattern found in everyday life. We see it in games like tic-tac-toe, in home décor, rugs and fabric, and even on our keyboards. It's child's play to color every block alternately.

The checkerboard is particularly dynamic in creating whimsical design. Added to spirals, stripes and dots, you have a festive set of canes.

The checkerboard stylizes the playful nature of these pins and paperweight by Barbara Mcguire.

Reversed Color Checkerboard Cane:

Reversing the colors can create exciting variations. Because of the contrast in value, this cane looks more like a plaid than a checkerboard.

- Prepare a shaded sheet of clay, 3 colors, lightest color in middle, largest thickness. Trim the sheet of clay to a rectangle, cut into 4 equal strips.
- Stack the strips, flipping the strips so the colors are reversed on the next sheet.

- Divide the stack in half and add both ends together keeping the sequence in order.
- Very carefully, making sure you are cutting straight down, slice downward on the stack, across the stripes. Each slice should be the same thickness as a layer of color.

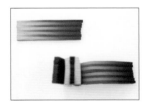 

- Restack the cut slices, reversing the color. When you align the slices, the stripes should be viewed as they are placed to guarantee perfect alignment.
- Slice through the middle of the cane to reveal the color pattern in the checkerboard. The color will change as you cut each slice.

Tips for Checkerboards

A checkerboard cane is made by slicing a striped stack evenly and flipping each striped section so it alternates colors as it is realigned. The sections should be cut the same thickness as the original sheets if the checkerboard is intended to be perfectly square.

Use high contrasting value in your colors. The checkerboard is a busy pattern and the colors will fight or blend if they are the same value.

The success of the checkerboard depends on slicing the slabs of stripe evenly. Bear down slowly and evenly on the blade as you slice, checking any variation in the

Graduated Color Checkerboard Cane

Graduatsing the colors can create exciting variations. Because of the contrast in value, this cane looks more like a plaid than a checkerboard.

- Prepare two sheets of shaded clay with the dark colors on one end. (In this example one of the sheets actually has the lightest color in the middle.) Stack the two sheets so the dark end of one sheet is next to the light end of the other sheet. Trim excess.
- Cut the stacked sheets into 4 sections across all the colors. Stack the sections.

- Cut across the short end of the cane into even slabs, the same thickness as the sheets, creating stripes. Invert alternating slices and reassemble to make a checkerboard. Trim the slices if they are not even.
- Note: Slicing machines are available to aid in measured slicing. This machine is called Precise a Slice.

The resulting checkerboard is very long and should be cut along the side of the cane. A good use for this cane would be borders or a bracelet.

direction of the blade constantly. Working in small portions helps to accomplish this, also making sure your sheets are consistent and matching thicknesses.

It may help to cool the stacks to firm the clay before you slice. Certain clays become soft as they are conditioned, and as a result, more difficult to control. The cane stacks can be placed briefly in the refrigerator for cooling.

Align the inverted (opposite color direction) slabs precisely as you restack the slabs. It feels like weaving as each stripe is placed next to the adjacent one.

Reduce the cane evenly to maintain the pattern of the checkerboard.

Flanking face canes with alternative borders helps determine future designs by Barbara McGuire.

Borders

Canes are often compiled to make borders or large sheets of pattern. Any cane in repetition can become a border, but one of my favorite sequences is a triangle border because it has great movement. The border illustrated is even more complicated because the sides of the triangles have drastically different values. This pulls the eye in one direction.

When slices are placed opposite each other, it creates a woven design similar to snake skin or fish scales. Although the colors used are rich, because I used mica clay, cutting across the cane darkened the colors because of the shift in the mica. I would recommend using opaque clay in my next attempt.

- Choose two 2" strips of blended color, light to dark.
- Roll each strip into a blended color bull's eye cane.
- Each bull's eye should be the same size in thickness and in length. Wrap one cane in White (thin) and one cane in Black (thinner)

Slice the through the canes vertically to make 6 sections (wedges) of each color. You may wish to do this first in halves, then in thirds. If the clay is soft and difficult to manage, firm by cooling in the refrigerator.

- Flatten each wedge into a triangle by pushing down (with your fingers) on the work surface on the outside edge (the Black or White) of the wedge.
- Align each triangle next to the alternate colored triangle, placing the triangles systematically so the White and Black edges create an alternate zigzag.

You will end up with points at each end. Flush cut one end and fill in the other, making the cane produce even edges so it can be joined.

Now the design can be reduced by stretching, rolling with a brayer and pulling.

- After a desirable reduction is reached, cut two slices of the cane and match them together, creating a diamond in the center.

Each slice of this cane pattern can be arranged to create a pattern sequence.

These lovely leaves by Carol Simmons are recognized by their shape as well as their color.

Different sizes of the same cane are helpful when rendering a design such as this stemmed flower by Barbara McGuire.

This incredible bouquet by Lynne Ann Schwarzenberg illustrates the true artistry of cane work.

Keeping several canes on hand helps an artist to choose the perfect collection of colors, as represented in this floral torpedo bead by Barbara McGuire.

Leaves

A simple shaded leaf is a highly versatile cane. The trick is to get the core bright enough to create dimension in the leaf. The color mix shown was reworked and modified several times before I was satisfied with the blend.

 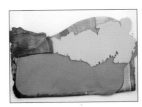 

Blend a sheet to make Green graduating from very light to dark.

Leaves with Veins

 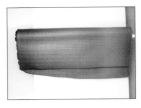 

• Keep modifying the blend, adding color or White until you are satisfied.
• Fold the blend in half, doubling the thickness. The additional thickness will make a more gradual highlight, and a wider (instead of longer) cane when rolling into a cylinder. This is helpful when slicing through the cane. Roll the doubled sheet into a blended cylinder, as shown in the project on page 9.
• Cut the cylinder in half though the face of the cane. Score and cut diagonal sections in one of the halves. Repeat on the opposite half, angling the cuts in reverse diagonals. These cuts create the veins. Place loosely on the work surface, but do not reassemble.

• Create a blended cylinder that will become the veins. This example shows a light Brown to Black cane. Cut a section of Brown cane the height of the Green cane, flatten and taper the section to become a middle vein. Reduce the remaining Brown cane and flatten and taper to a smaller proportion than the middle vein.
• Insert the smaller veins between the diagonal sections.
• When one side is reassembled, add the middle vein.

• Complete the opposite side and join the 2 halves, aligning the veins.
• Reduce the cane by stroking and pulling and tapering the cane into a teardrop. The ends become handles as the cane is pulled. I prefer to reduce the cane in various sizes to create a variety of leaf sizes.

Striped Leaf

Bold graphic leaves stand out in a design. These leaves are enhanced because each section between the lines is shaded from light to dark. This is a classic example of how to make a short transition from dark to light in a large volume of clay within a small space.

- Begin with a blended sheet on the thickest setting.
- Section the sheet into strips, beginning with a light strip and ending with a dark strip.

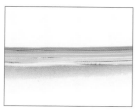 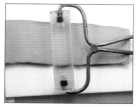

- Stack the strips from light to dark.
- Flatten the entire sheet, which will also expand and elongate the sheet. You can also run the sheets through the pasta machine to accomplish this.

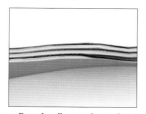 

- Cut the flat end stack into sections and assemble in layers, one on top of the other.
- Cut the stacked sections into even portions and restack the cane to create a block of stripes.

- Place the cane stack on its side, stripes facing upward, and slice in half, and then diagonally at a 45° angle. • Position the cut sections along the diagonals, aligning the inside seam to make a downward V – but do not join!

- Insert a vein (as illustrated in the previous projects) into the middle of the leaf cane. Trim the sides to even the shape of the cane. • Reduce the cane by pulling and stretching, in diminishing size so you have a variety of leaf sizes when the cane is sliced.

Palm Leaf

The palm is another way to get veins in a leaf. The added attraction is that the cane itself has an organic shape if it can be reduced by stretching. This shape can also be intensified or redefined in each slice before it is utilized in a project.

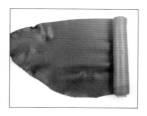  

- Create a blended roll cane with a light core and a dark outer edge.
- Reduce the roll to several diameters, diminishing in size.
- Use a brayer to taper the rolls, tilting to one side to pinch the cane into a teardrop shape.

  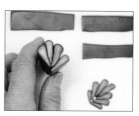

- If you experience an air bubble when tapering, slice through it on the side of the bubble and smooth the clay together to patch the hole.
- Cut into 7 sections, the largest is the middle and 3 pairs of diminishing diameters, each section the same size. The cross sections will form a palm leaf.
- Assemble the sections together in diminishing sizes, joining the points to each other as shown.

- Reduce the cane by stroking and pulling, trying to handle the cane so the individual leaves do not distort. The ends become handles as the cane is pulled. I prefer to reduce the cane in various sizes to create a variety of leaf sizes.
- When applying the cane to a design, you can reshape the slices with a needle tool to define the shape of the slice.

continued on page 18...

continued from page 17...

Holly Leaf

The shape of a leaf can be very subtle but defining. Here the edges point outward in spikes.

To retain those spikes, the cane is made with an outer blanket of translucent clay which also helps to create the shape of the leaf. The translucent will clear during baking, and the spiky leaf will be defined.

This is a classic example of how to keep a sharp edge in the outline of a cane. Since the middle of the cane is opaque, the challenge will also be to slice as thin as possible so the translucent will clear, leaving the opaque clay most visible.

• Begin with a cylinder of shaded clay – shown here, the core is darker than the outer edge. It is easier to work with a short stack. Cut the stack in half and then shape the half into a teardrop.
• Make small 'snakes' of translucent clay and press into the sides of the teardrop. The pressure exerted as you press the snakes into the sides will force the teardrop to spike along the outer edges.

• Add more translucent snakes to completely cover the outer sides of the teardrop.
• Once the cane is assembled, you can carve away the ridges on the outer sides to create a leaf shape while retaining the intended design in the leaf. This method of carving away instead of forcing together is a fundamental concept to keeping integrity in your shapes.

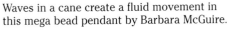
Waves in a cane create a fluid movement in this mega bead pendant by Barbara McGuire.

Waves

There are lots of tools to use in shaping and cutting such as the wavy blade.

This blade was originally used for cutting French fries and was adopted by the polymer artists, so look frequently for tools from unique sources. Several versions of the blade are available, so be sure your wave has the desired rhythm.

• Roll a short and wide blended cylinder. A wide shape is easier to cut through than a long thin one. • Cut across the cylinder with the wavy blade, fanning the cuts out from the center cut as shown. • Using sections cut from another light color shaded cylinder, flatten the sections from dark to light and place them between the wave cuts. • Use a tube to help push the light color tightly into the wave cuts without distorting the cut. Reassemble, keeping the portions in sequence, as they are easily mixed up.

• Trim excess flaps of color that extend past the cane edge. • Bend a flexible blade to cut a curve at the bottom of the fan. • Insert a small blended cylinder into the bottom of the fan and pull the cane around it.

Petals

The petals of a flower are a trademark of cane work. The name millefiori means 'thousand flowers' in Italian where the technique was made popular with glass trade beads 2,000 years ago.

The variations on a petal cane are infinite and specific color palettes will distinguish a collection of flower canes.

Tips for Petals

The number of petals in the complete flower is an added variable to a design. Make large amounts of cane so you can experiment with the number and shape of petals.

Wrapping petals in a color makes the background color encircle the flower design. The only time it 'melts' into the background is when it is the same color as the background.

If you do not wrap a petal cane completely, but only fill in the space in-between petals, when sliced and applied as millefiori, the edges of the slice will look like stripes.

Surrounding a petal cane with translucent clay will allow the cane to 'float' when it is used in a design. The translucent will clear as it bakes, taking on the color of the background.

Outlining in White is just as effective as Black.

Create registration marks when you have a petal that has stamens. It's important to align the petals so that all the flower centers are radiating outward, not crooked.

High contrast petals will reduce well. Opaque clay works best to retain the contrast. Translucent clay petals will diminish in impact as they are reduced because the clay will clear to some extent. Pearl and metallic clay may reflect darker when the petals are cut across the grain,

Flower canes serve as exceptional borders.

This modern version of classic millefiori (meaning a thousand flowers) is presented by Petra Nieuwenhuize.

Begin with color: Prepare a large thick blended bull's eye of the color of choice - usually a bright light color at the core, blending to an outer darker color. The outline of your petal will most likely depend on the core colors. Prepare thin sheets of Black and White clay, as well as condition translucent clay for packing the cane after it is assembled.

• Slice the bull's eye in half, across the length of the cane. Use a metal tube, a wooden stick, or some tool to indent a circle into the center of the cane. • Roll the Black and White sheets very thin and stack them together. Fold over to make a 'sandwich' with Black on the outside and White in the middle. This will become the stamen. • Trim and wedge one edge if desired.

• Roll a small Black cylinder of clay and place it in the indent. Adjust the size to fit. Place the stamen on one half of the cane touching the center cylinder. Place the two halves of the cane back together, aligning the colors and edges.
• Wrap the cane in a thin sheet of White, beginning at the stamen. Trim and join the sheet exactly, do not overlap the sheet.
• Wrap the sheet in Black, leaving a small gap where it should be joined. This gap is to serve as a registration mark for aligning the petals. The illustration shows a plug placed into the cane end to prepare for reduction. As the cane is reduced, the outer layers of clay will envelope over the plug and reduce the cane more evenly.

• Reduce the cane, pinch into a teardrop shape by pinching on one side of the cylinder.
• Cut the teardrop cane into 5 equal lengths and wrap each section with a sheet of translucent clay. Note: this step can also be done before reduction.

continued on page 20

continued from page 19...

• Make a bull's eye of Black and White and reduce to a size appropriate as a flower center. Assemble the sections upright around the center with all the points radiating outward. Note: The translucent wrap has begun to split in one spot. This needs to be smoothed over before continuing. • Check the symmetry of the aligned petals at both ends before you begin to pack the cane. Roll a cylinder of translucent clay and divide into sections like a pie. Pinch and place translucent sections to fit in-between the petals.

• Wrap the entire cane with translucent.
• Place additional portions of clay next to each petal where the translucent is lacking. This is so the shape of the petal is retained. Clay will flow into any open space, changing the shape of the petals, so it is important that spaces are filled.

Petals do not have to be flowers or daisies! There are petals in the neck adornment of the Egyptian image by Barbara McGuire. Notice the use of checkerboard and stripes for the hair.

The background of a petal will appear as a circle surrounding the flower, as illustrated in beads by Barbara McGuire.

Spliced Petals

This cane reminds me of folding my hands in prayer – it's good to find something that you can relate to visually to help you build the cane. I often refer to sections in an orange, or 'making a burrito' as a reference to help to explain the jump from the physical construction of a cane to the 2 dimensional surface designs it creates.

The added beauty of this cane is that it is random and flowing, and even the pinched ends can be used in the final assembly.

Petals in a square cane create a simple pattern for this matchbox pendant by Barbara McGuire.

MATERIALS:
Basic tools • Blended sheet with light colors (including White), value from dark to light, rolled into a bull's eye cane. The bull's eye should be a wide stocky cane.

• Slice the bull's eye vertically through the cane (like a pie) into 8 sections. Pinch or Roll each section flat (about $\frac{1}{16}$" with the high value on one side and the low value on the other. Taper the edges of the sections by tilting the brayer as you roll to reshape the cane. Set aside the sections in two groups of four, each group with the light color facing the middle. • Assemble the sections, overlapping and intersecting the light edges in the middle. • The cane will resemble a melon, thick and light in the middle and dark on the edges.

When you reduce the cane, leave one end large and reduce the other to a diminishing size. This gives you a variety of sizes to create a flower.

Petals illustrate radial symmetry in cane designs by Barbara McGuire. The background is as important in the design as the focus.

The Rose

As complicated as it looks, the rose is one of the easiest canes to make because it is a replication of one cane. The distortions or variables of the one cane will enhance shapes. Color is a key factor, with dynamic effects stemming from high contrast.

Kim Korringa shapes individual cane slices to add shape to petals.

Tips for Making a Rose

Refer to a picture of a 'real' rose when viewing shapes. Mimicry of the shape will greatly enhance the cane.

Prepare leaves in advance, to use with a number of applications. Try on several 'leaves' before you decide which one is appropriate.

Don't be intimidated by the look of the final outcome – This cane is easy!

Soften the translucent clay that surrounds the rose thoroughly, it will stretch easier when conditioned well.

A rose with a solid background (instead of translucent) will look like a rose in a circle when used in a project.

Color: I rarely blend Orange into Magenta, because the Orange dominates (due to intense saturation of color) and Magenta is nearly lost; however, it is still detectable to the eye. • Therefore, I repeated Magenta in the spiked rays that extend out into the petal, which next to White and Yellow, are an adequate contrast and pick up Magenta in the rim.
• Prepare a large blended bull's eye with the lightest color at the core. Reduce and cut the cane into 3" lengths of various diameters.

• Divide each section into two halves, cutting lengthwise through the cane. Pinch the sides of canes to fashion each section into a petal. The goal is to spread the half circle, tapering the sides and leaving a thicker middle. Make a very thin sheet of magenta clay to lay on top of each half.
• Use a bone folder to randomly press the magenta strip into the half cane sections. Press deeply, and check your results by slicing off an end, viewing the effects of the magenta in the cross section. Each cane section should have a variable spiked result, adding to the variety of the petals. • Assemble the petal sections around each other, beginning with the smallest section and working to the larger sections as you rotate around the flower. The smallest section will begin almost as a spiral, as it turns around itself. • When the rose is completed, insert a few small leaves in between the outer petals. • Begin to fill in the negative space (the air) around the rose cane.

• Use quartered cylinders and sheets of clay to fill the gaps, retaining the shape of the rose. • When needed, press into the crevices to fill all the gaps using various tools such as a bone folder. • Slice an end to reveal the rose pattern. I often save these ends as references. • Reduce the rose by squeezing at the core of the cane. • Reduce the rose in various diameters so you have a bouquet!

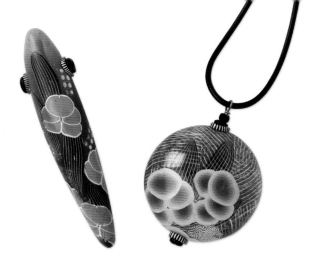

Donna Kato utilizes translucent color in her trademark imagery and cane work.

Delicate swirls of color are embedded under layers of flowing translucent lines to create these wonderfully appealing beads and bracelet by Karen Lewis.

Translucent and White Canes

Translucent canes are mesmerizing because translucent clay clears to a great extent in baking, leaving the outline of any pattern of opaque color built into the cane. The key is slicing the translucent layers extremely thin, so the clay will actually clear.

It is also popular to overlap these types of cane, creating layers of depth.

Tips for Translucents

Outline translucent canes in White. If you outline in Black, you will see through the edge of the cane, causing the translucent clay to appear dirty.

You can tint the translucent clay to any color, but it only requires a very small dot of color to change the entire block of translucent clay.

Translucent clay can appear as stone and is desirable for certain 'old world' looks.

Generally translucent clay is a different consistency than opaque clay – it can feel rubbery and resistant to reduction by splitting. Some brands also 'plaque' which means the clay has little fractions that resemble bubbles or cracks. This can also occur with excessive conditioning. Test your brand for particularities.

The key is making canes that are easily sliced thin. Square and rectangle canes cane be more controllable in slicing. They are usually sliced across, with the cane pointing upward.

Explore simple graphic patterns in White and translucent canes. These are incredibly effective as a line element in an overall design.

Chrissy Cane

The Chrissy cane is short for chrysanthemum, the flower it mimics. The cane employs a simple 'adjustment' to a translucent spiral. Here it is illustrated both in translucent and shaded translucent Chrissy canes. The translucent clay creates the illusion of depth in the layers because you are looking through the translucent to the White folds (rings) when the cane is viewed. This also works in reverse, when the outline color is dark, for example Black, the cane will have a shaded depth. I find the White outline to be more attractive in this cane.

This cane is effective with very thin slices and overlaps in the final design.

• Condition the translucent clay and roll into a flat sheet. Condition the White clay and roll into a thin flat sheet. Your goal is to have the outline delicate, so a thinner sheet will enhance this effect. Lay the two sheets together and trim.
• Begin to make a jelly roll. As you roll, push the side of the credit card or bone folder into the side of inside cane lengthwise, making ridges; continue rolling and making ridges each turn.
• Eventually you will be making ridges in the entire cane. Reduce the cane on one end, leaving options for variable sizes. Note: a variation of this method is to roll the clay into a jelly roll and then push into the side of the cane to make ridges.

Shaded Chrissy Cane

The instructions for the shaded cane are the same as above, only the translucent sheet is tinted into a blend. This can be done by adding tiny TINY bits of color to translucent clay. • The illustration shows adding an entire strip of color, taken from a blended sheet, and added to a sheet of translucent clay. • The sheet is trimmed and stacked with a very thin White layer. • It is rolled and pressed with a bone folder as it is assembled.

Kim Cavender creates a delightful bracelet with this theme of translucent cane work. The shiny finishing on this piece reflects sanding and polishing to perfection, adding sophistication and refinement to the work.

Large sheets of translucent cane surface design are cropped with templates to create these fabulous earring shapes by Petra Nieuwenhuize.

Some translucent can appear as stone, as illustrated in this journal cover by Barbara McGuire.

This delightful doll by Petra Nieuwenhuize illustrates an inventive use of translucent canes.

Floating Carpet

This cane illustrated the simplicity of repeating a graphic design to create a field of pattern. There is not a lot of translucent clay in the design, but the squares will appear to float when the cane is cured.

The squares can also be reduced to different shapes, such as rectangles or even dashes.

• Prepare both White and translucent clay in sheets. Stack sheets of White clay and trim to make a square cane. slicing the edges will retain a sharp crisp square.
• Wrap the square with translucent, a very thin sheet of White, and again translucent. The fact that you will be placing the translucent next to another translucent cane will actually double the amounts of translucent.
• Reduce by rolling each side of the square cane with a brayer. Be sure to flip and rotate the cane as you roll. Notice all the squares are not perfect because different pressure was applied in reduction. Cut the strips into 4 portions and assemble next to each other.
• Cut the assembled cane into 4 sections and restack. Align the cane as evenly as possible to make a field of pattern, similar to a quilt.
• The finished cane should be packed together and if there is any portion left over, it can be further reduced and made into another cane of thinner dimension.

White Spirals

The key to this design is in the assembly of differing sizes of spirals and the direction they are winding. It takes a lot of canes to make a field. It is also important that the cane are aligned so they do not distort each other.

• Create several spirals with White outline and a translucent outside. This is done by embedding the layer of White clay between two layers of translucent. This preserves the integrity of the White line.
• Assemble the canes with the spiral turning in different directions, and different sizes aligned next to each other. The field of spirals will be large enough to slice very thin as the cane is standing upright.

Sketches of Cane Ideas

It is a good idea to sketch out rough ideas for canes. Even though you may not follow the sketch exactly, at least you'll have a starting point.

These drawings show sketches of canes before beginning to create them.

Line drawings are an excellent tool in preparing to design a cane. Look for inspiration from fabric design, rugs, knobs, tiles, finials and ethnic patterns. Many of these drawings were inspired by middle eastern henna designs.

Reduction of Invisible Canes

A cane is easiest to reduce when it is pliable; however, it can be too soft as well, and need to sit, or in some cases – refrigerate - for a while to make it reduce evenly.

• Begin by pinching the cane with your fingers into the shape you wish - square or triangle.

• Use a roller to stretch the cane, turning it on each side clockwise and pulling to stretch it as you roll across it. Flip it end to end and roll & pull again, this time turning the cane counterclockwise as you stretch. This helps the cane to reduce evenly without bearing more weight or pressure on one or another side. Important! Reduction can blur the mica shift, because it begins to recomb the mica. The most predominant variations are cut across the layers.

Invisible Canes

Canes can appear as shadows, a technique interpreted by Dan Cormier.

The phenomenon of light refraction is experienced in the invisible canes. The term invisible comes from the fact that the clay is all one color, and it is the alignment of the cuts that create the allusion of color value. These canes are subtle and are most effective when made using highly metallic or pearl colors. The canes also appear to float against a solid sheet, and the reflected light creates dimension.

Invisible Quilt Canes

• Cut one mica striped square stack from corner to corner. This makes 4 triangles. Repeat the process with the other square striped stack.

• Place two triangles together so the stripes align perpendicular on the longest side of the triangle. This makes a small square. Place all four squares together, the resulting alignments will produce a concentric square or a radiant diamond.

MATERIALS:
Basic tools
Metallic or Pearl clay that has mica in it.

• Condition the color by running sheets through the pasta machine in a continuous direction. This combs the mica in one direction.

• Cut the sheet into strips and stack – do not change any direction in stacking the clay. The stacks need to be as tall as they are wide so divide the stack in half and stack to make a large chunky rectangle. Cut this rectangle to produce two square blocks. • Arrange one block so it reflects a lighter value (the sheets stacked as they were run through the pasta machine) and the other block with the cut side face up. • Slice even slabs through each square of color. Here the slices are shown using a wavy blade. • Reassemble the cane, alternating the light value and dark value slices.

Dragonfly

Making a representative cane is merely a matter of patience and interpretation. You can create as complicated and exact of a cane as you have patience for, but that may not be any more effective than a simple cane that is representational of an object.

In the long run, the truth is, the clay is vulnerable to distortion - sometimes because of the softness of the clay, other times because of the gaps between layers, or the pressures applied during reduction.

Always keep in mind that distortion is a possibility. In most cases, this creates a more artistic representation, instead of a rigid graphic representation. In a rigid design, the mistakes will pop out. In an interpretive design, the loss of control can become an enhancement.

Design your canes with a flair for interpretation. The cane cannot be judged for its right or wrong, but its inherent beauty.

Tips for Realistic Canes

Analyze the essence of your design. In looking at the dragonfly wings, as well as butterfly wings, I noticed a repetition of long narrow shapes, and little dots. In planning, seek the essence of the design and focus on mimicking those features.

Although I actually built this cane spontaneously, because though experience I am able to visualize and assemble shapes, I have drawn a line pattern so the reader is able to understand the shapes I am manipulating to make the cane.

Look at photos of objects and samples of cane work by others as references during the entire building process.

Use color to mimic design as well as shapes. For example, a green leaf will look more like a leaf than a stack of stripes if it is green.

Wrap sections to retain the integrity of the shapes. This also prevents spider veins where sheets of clay join.

Use tools to manipulate shapes, remember each positive shape must have its surrounding (negative) counterpart. If the two shapes are not matches, they will 'move' into place changing shapes of the sections.

Outline specific areas with fine lines in both Black and White for dimensional contrast.

Include high and low values for dynamic dimension.

Plan the background as thoroughly as the design.

Create icons you will use often. I once made a cactus – it really had limitations to southwest themes.

Create an incredible cane at least once in your life.

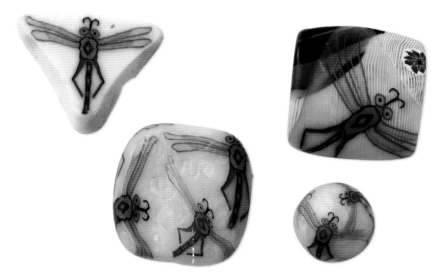

One cane goes a long way in different designs. Canes can be stored for many years, however its flexibility may diminish. A cane is best used soon after it is created.

- Prepare colors. In this example, the colors are somewhere between natural and bright. There is a full range of light to dark in each blend.
- Three colors are created, a White to Black (for wing lines), a White to Gold (for wing body), and a Red to White (for dots on wings).
- Note: You will be making one wing and reduce and split it into two large wings and two small wings.

- Slice through and manipulate the lightest of the shaded cylinders into sections that will create the main bulk of the wings.
- Reduce the Black shaded bull's eye to 8 sections. Flatten, press and pinch each of these sections into strips that will interlock to make veins in the wings.
- Prepare Red dots to go in-between the veins at midpoint of the wing.

- Placing the shapes together calls for manipulating each shape and joining it exactly with the adjacent shape. Because the fingers are bulky for detail, frequently use tools such as brass rods to help make curves.
- Dots and several veins are bent into arches, as they interlock to build the design.
- This method of using a tool to shape layers will help to keep the series of dots along the bottom of the wing circular as layers are added and the cane is packed.

continued on page 26...

continued from page 25...

Representational images are built with imagination and flair as reflected in this design by Marie Segal.

• The body of the fly is built using colors in the wings. Here a strip is inserted to make a line in the middle of the Black cylinder.
• Smaller shapes are interlocked to make the tail.

 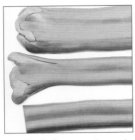 

• When the components are finished, they can be reduced proportionately. This is done by pressing, and pulling. The ends will be similar to handles that enable you to pull the cane like taffy, keeping as much as possible of the original wing shape.
• A final summation or mock-up is done with slices to see if there is anything to change or add to the cane before it is wrapped. Notice the reject of options such as the colors of the eyes, which were too bright (in White) for my taste.

• Wrap each section with translucent to keep the sections intact and prevent interruption in the edges. • Assemble the sections for packing.
• The space around the cane is the negative space. Begin to pack the cane by inserting matching shapes of translucent clay into the negative space.
• These shapes can also be manipulated with tools to assist the match.

Themed canes enhance this collection by Barbara McGuire. When building canes that employ shapes that represent images, the negative space around the image must be considered to maintain the shape of the image.

• Trim ends so you can see what you are doing, and also so you can recycle the excess clay.
• Continually fill in gaps without changing the position or shapes of the design. Wrap in layers when possible.
• When the cane is completely packed, trim evenly on the outside.
• If the cane is not flush on the outside edge, the reduction will 'bump' all the clay inside, distorting the design.

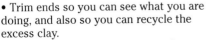

Designing the cane is just a small part of designing the overall piece. All the components should complement the focus. Memory Wire Choker with antique buttons by Barbara McGuire.

A collection of image canes can coordinate together to make a complete theme. Be sure you create themes you will actually wear.

Reduction of a Dragonfly

When reducing a cane it is imperative that the design be moved as a whole. It can be difficult to reduce a large cane because you simply can't grab it, or the mass is too thick to move.

I used a method of banging or smacking the cane against a hard surface to get the initial mass to move. Once it is manageable, stretch it in more coaxing means.

Tips for Reduction

Be sure the outer sides are flush, as the clay will bump all the packed inside pieces together.

Wrap canes with lots of outer layers so distortion of inner layers is less.

Work on firm surfaces with clean hands.

Let the cane set before reduction if it is too squishy to hold the lines of the design.

Rotate and flip to apply pressures equally.

Squeeze from the middle, pulling to the outer edges.

Use tools such as a brayer, or an acrylic rolling plate instead of fingers.

Cut and review portions before assuming a cane has reduced well. I have often reduced a cane too much.

• Hold the cane above a firm surface on a sturdy table, bang the entire side down on the table with great force. Rotate the cane and repeat for each side in a clockwise direction. • Repeat applying force on all sides, this time moving in a counterclockwise direction. • Flip the cane (right to left and repeat the above steps. It is necessary to rotate and flip because the cane will 'inch' in one direction due to the force exerted by your right or left hand.

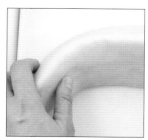 

• Eventually the cane will soften and become more flexible, You can flex the cane back and forth as you pull and coax it into a smaller dimension.
• As the cane becomes smaller, you should stop and slice a portion off the end to check the reduction.

• Some canes are only effective to a certain point and actually lose effect if reduced too small.

Reduction is a challenge to maintain the line in a design. There are many ways to reduce a cane, including this tricky method of attaching each end of the cane to a slick surface and pulling the cane into a small diameter. The reward is a more accurate reduction and less waste in the process.

This cane was reduced in varying stages to accommodate the large amount of work surrounding the actual face cane.

It was more difficult to reduce because of the face not being a straight on view.

The deeper the face is embedded in the middle of the cane, the less chance of distortion.

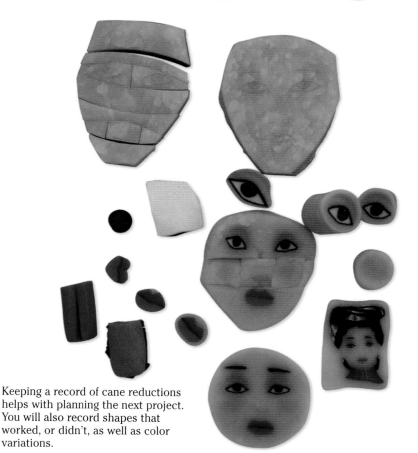

Keeping a record of cane reductions helps with planning the next project. You will also record shapes that worked, or didn't, as well as color variations.

Store face canes in deli wrap, in a cool dark place to increase longevity.

Faces

I have always been attracted to faces. The face is the most expressive means of identity and communication we possess.

These canes are simply assembled colors and shapes of clay, but have taken on the representation of a being. Even cartoon faces have an expressive quality. To enable handling of the fine detail, it is easier to construct a huge face and reduce it, which is the 'trick' to those 'tiny' faces. Creating a portrait in clay takes patience, careful observation and willingness to persevere to a final outcome. It also takes applied and concentrated judgments.

Your reward is a unique piece of artistry that lasts for years.

Illustrations on tracing paper are the first step in effective face canes.

The graphite image is transferred to the clay and serves as a guide throughout the entire process.

• Size your picture to the exact size you will be making the cane. Shape translucent Flesh to the face in the picture.

• Trace your picture, outlining features with a soft pencil, trace again on back of tracing paper. Image is now facing correct way. Place drawing on translucent clay, rub with a bone folder. This transfers graphite to clay and serves as a guide for building a cane. Set aside while you build the features of the face.

• Build features and size them according to the drawing, cut out a corresponding section in face and replace the cut area with built features.

Mixing Colors for the Face

• **Mixing color** is paramount in making face-sand it is recommended to use translucent clay.

Translucent clay blends together in shades instead of defined opaque 'sections'. The color you choose will reflect ethnic identities. First mix the opaque colors in complete ranges, light, medium, dark as well as color for eyes, cheeks and lips. Use small amounts of opaque clay to tint a whole pound of translucent clay.

It's challenging to know how deeply you have colored translucent clay, so I suggest holding a thin portion of translucent up to the light to look at the color as a test or bake a test sample of clay. The final goal is to make a translucent cane that will be thinly sliced and backed on a layer of White. This is how you get the luminosity or soft glowing appeal to the cane.

• **Start with a base color** such as Flesh, Beige or Ecru and add tiny bits of Burnt Sienna, Red, Copper or Pink, -even Blue or White to get a flesh you like. Divide the color into three parts Lighten 1/3 portion with White and darken 1/3 portion with Sienna (or Brown). Use the same Red for the lips as the cheeks, etc. – remain consistent within the color palette.

Use the same Brown throughout the face – ie – to darken the flesh and also for the brow. I rarely use straight Black except for the pupils in the eyes and the top eye line.

The lower lip color should be slightly lighter than the upper lip color. Colors such as the White for the eyes, the iris, the brow, lips and outline clays are not translucent tints – they are opaque colors with bits of translucent for consistency.

Once you have made this base range of color – you can use it to tint the translucent. That will be the bulk of the face. Tint 3/4 lb. of translucent clay with the mid range flesh. Use only a 1" diameter ball to tint the entire pound. Adjust accordingly -if the color is too faint, add more flesh. If you want a darker flesh, add more flesh.

Mix remaining translucent with light and dark flesh. Keep all these colors in order so you won't get confused.

• **Size your picture** to the exact size you will be making the cane. Shape the translucent flesh to the face of the picture. Trace the picture, outlining the features with pencil, trace again on the back of the tracing paper (otherwise the image would be reversed).

Place the drawing on the translucent clay and rub with a bone folder. This transfers the graphite to the clay and serves as a guide for building the cane. Set this aside while you build the features of the face.

You will build these features and size them according to the drawing, then cut out a corresponding section in the face and replace the cut area with the built features.

For Eyes

- You have to begin somewhere, so start with the eye. Every detail counts, so use a shaded blend for the iris of the eye. Roll the blend into a cylinder with the light in the middle. Slice the top ⅓ part of the cylinder horizontally. This is to insert the pupil. Make an indent with the cylinder tool to accept the pupil. Place a snake of Black clay into the indent for the pupil. Slice to even the top of the eye. Indent a ridge to accept the gleam of the eye.
- This is a White 'dot' that rests at the top of each eye. We will be making one big eye and stretching it into two eyes. Keep in mind the gleam will represent reflection of light, and should be at the same placement in each eye. Therefore, due to possible distortion, it is best to keep the gleam at the center top. Throughout the entire process, we will indent or create the space for the next shape to fit into. Insert the gleam of the eye. In this example, the iris is completed, but it is also possible to place the cut section of iris back into the eye. Each eye is unique. Compare it to the drawing – is the eye round? It usually is cut off at the top by the lid. Notice these small details throughout the process.

In this pin by Barbara McGuire, a small slice of cane is framed as a focus. The cane slice has been backed with White clay to illuminate the translucent clay.

- Begin to shape pieces for the corners or the Whites of the eyes. These are typically triangles but have very subtle convex or concave curves.

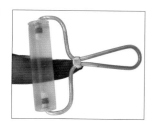

- Look very closely at your sketch or picture and create exactly the shapes you see, not what you think you see. Use tools to help create the shapes.
- Place the whites of the eyes at the sides of the iris.
- Now we will build the shading around the eyes.
- Wrap this entire unit in flesh color, in this case a dark flesh because this will soften the transition of color around the eye.
- Create a lash line by tapering a slab of brown to fit over the top of the eye.

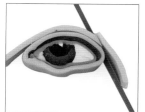

- Place clay slab so the thickest part of the lash line rests at the outer corner of the eye.
- Wrap the entire eye in flesh. This "wrapping" is to encase the eye so there is a continuous wrap to create a smooth outline.
- If pieces were added by section, it is possible that small bits of clay would 'leak in' between the sections. This wrapping of the features is done consistently throughout the cane.
- Add another layer of flesh color to account for a thick lid. Trim the layer to taper at the corners. Add a darker layer to account for a lid crease, again trim the edges. • Wrap the eye in flesh again. This creates bulk to the cane, and embeds the eye design deeply into the center, so when you place it in the face, the eye has less of a probability of distortion. Your eye should be long enough to make two units of eye. Stretching the eye is necessary to fit the proportion to the drawing. Cut a piece from both ends to make sure everything is in place. I usually save these pieces as references. Compare the eye to the original drawing. Note: The second eye will be the cane turned around, because the smaller whites will be on the inside of both eyes. It is important that the gleam remain centered or directed towards the same side.

continued on page 30...

continued from page 29...

For the Whole Face

• Now you are going to cut into the whole face to section it, and remove and replace sections. First cut out square sections for the eyes. • Add triangle shapes of clay (slice the clay corners from the area you cut out) and make a square section of eye to insert. Trim the eye to fit exactly and make sure both eyes are aligned correctly, both front and back.

• Prepare two strips of brown clay to be 'eyebrows'. Taper one edge of the strip so the eyebrows once placed, will be thick at the bridge of the nose, and thin towards the outside of the brow. Wrap the brow in flesh. • Place a crescent shape (sliced from removed brow) over the eye and place brow on top of eye.

• Place the eyes and brow into the spaces created for the eye sections. Take the forehead section and carve out the area for the brow by bending blade and carving down. (Use a flexible blade.) Smooth the inside of holes before you replace the forehead. • Adjust any and all portions as you reassemble the cane.

• Details of the lips are just as important as the eyes.

• Make lips by cutting a shaded bull's eye into 2 half circles (lengthwise).

• The top should be slightly smaller than the bottom. Taper both sides of the halves to create corners of the mouth.

• The lower lip has an indent in the middle and the upper lip has a ridge to allow for the curve of the smile line. Use tools to shape each of these parts before placing them together.

• Place an extremely thin sheet of brown clay between the lips to define the smile line.

• Dent the upper lip to create the definition of the upper lips.

• Trim any 'smile line' clay. Wrap the entire unit in flesh clay.

• Add a tiny triangle of flesh clay into the dent in the upper lip to keep this area defined. Note: Anytime you use clay from an 'extracted' portion – remember to remove the graphite so it doesn't discolor the cane. Compare the lips with the picture of your face cane and stretch to proper proportion.

This face cane by Barbara McGuire is cropped to present an interestingly shaped bead.

Slice canes as thin as possible and with as little pressure bearing down as possible, by cutting across the cane.

Acknowledgements & Dedication

Cane making is thousands of centuries old. It is simultaneously technical and interpretive. Something borrowed, something new, something old, and something blue, it continues on through generations of creative hands. I wish to thank Suzanne McNeil for enabling this information to be recorded in time and physically shared.

I commend my friends and peers who have allowed me to experience their discoveries, particularly Judith Skinner, Sarah Shriver, Karen Lewis, Donna Kato, and Valerie Wright. I hope that we will never hold back in dispersing the skills and innovations that challenge the mind and enlighten the soul.

This book is dedicated to Margaret Kolk and Chris Truhe, owners of Carisma Gallery, whose dedication and support of artists has been a constant and unwavering inspiration.

Barbara McGuire

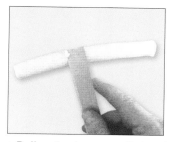

- Roll a cheek cane to fit into both cheeks. If there are air bubbles, slice into the cane at an angle to release air and smooth the cane.
- Place cane, reassemble face. Pack the cane together as before.

These beads show the effects of varying skin tones used in a face cane.

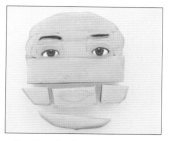

- Section the face to accommodate the lips. Remove the lips section and build up the lips to replace the entire mouth.
- Once the face is put back together – we are going to cut it apart for the nose. The 'hole' will help us to determine the size of the nose. Make it a little smaller than you think, because in reduction, it is the nose that stretches the least.

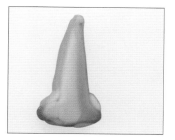
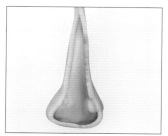

- A nose is not 'Black' - but a combination of light and dark shades of flesh. The nose shape is awkward to make – but just start by making a triangle – this nose had $\frac{1}{2}$ light flesh and $\frac{1}{2}$ dark flesh, according to the shadows in the original picture. This cane did not have darkened nostrils, but relies on the shape of the outline to define the 'bulb' of the nose and the nostrils.
- Wrap the entire unit in flesh, as you have done with the other features and reduce to size for insertion. Smooth out the crevice for the nose in the shape you are going to insert.

Translucent faces will require an under layer of White clay to bring out the luminescence. Here the faces on White are stored in between two layers of heavy plastic.

For Cheeks

This example does not illustrate cheeks, but they are created and inserted exactly as the other features. They will add dimension to a face if done in a light color, but they will paint a face cartoonish if the cheeks are too dark.

Directions: Make the cheeks with a slightly deep end or pinker color of flesh, blending into the flesh color of your face. Be very careful not to make the cheeks too rosy. Remember you will need two cheeks and roll into a shaded cylinder that has the darkest color in the middle and blends outward to flesh. The gradual blend makes the cheeks rosy and contours the face.

Section the face for cheeks, being very careful not to slice into any of the other features. Sometimes this can be done by punching out a 'cheek' circle with a clean large brass tube just under the eyes. Scrape the inside of the hole to make sure there are no residues of brass, and the inside is smooth.

Roll the cheek cane to fit into both cheeks. Place the cane and reassemble the face. Pack the cane together as before.

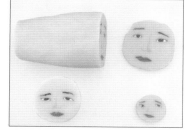

- Reassemble the face and press together. Wrap it entirely with translucent clay until all the features are well inside the edge of the cane. This adds extra clay on the outside which is probable to stretch. • Piece it together and pack firmly by 'whacking' it on all sides. Rotate and turn so the pressure of you pushing it together is distributed throughout the cane and you are not heavy on your strongest hand. (See instructions for reduction.) Slice across the top – and you will see the beautiful face underneath.

Sarah Shriver is a genius at creating Kaleidoscope patterns. A small portion of an original cane can be cut and reassembled to create inventive symmetry.

Differing sizes and arrangements create a unified presentation when making collections such as these eggs by Barbara McGuire.

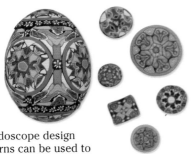

Kaleidoscope design patterns can be used to decorate many objects, including this egg by Barbara McGuire.

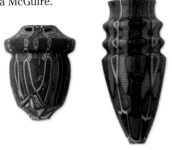

Canes can be turned and carved on a lathe into interesting shapes revealing color patterns as illustrated in these collaborative beads by Norm Robinson and Barbara McGuire.

A Single Kaleidoscope bead by Barbara Mcguire is captured dramatically in this elegant wirework necklace by Lisa Barth.

Kaleidoscope Canes

The premise of designing patterns is to repeat a shape in a consistent manner creating rhythm. This becomes more complex when the shapes are mirrored, waved or placed adjacent to the original design in such a manner that the touching borders also create shapes and patterns. With canes this process is delightful as each slice affords the opportunity to be reshaped or recut into a new motif.

Many people have experienced viewing through a kaleidoscope, a cylindrical toy that crops and mirrors the view of illuminated shapes and colors to make complex patterns. Artist Sarah Shriver has mastered a process to create awesome and inspiring art that resembles the designs created with a kaleidoscope. Sarah excels at teaching this process and the following example is a set of canes that were designed for her classes.

Tips for Kaleidoscope Canes

Make the original cane extremely large – Nearly a pound of clay!

Keep the shapes and designs large and simple.

Outline the shapes with high and low values.

Shade the shapes using blends and splices.

Keep in mind that a cane can be cropped or reshaped to make different combinations of shapes. Inserting additional shapes as you design is also an option.

Use bright, clean colors.

Avoid placing colors that have the same value next to each other. Contrast is key.

A spiral in the design helps to create detail.

Do not try to anticipate the results – instead, assemble and reshape the cane into patterns you would never dream of. Use end pieces to work out the details of the pattern before you reassemble all the canes.

Old canes can be reborn in this process by cutting and reassembling.

Pay attention! These assemblages can easily get reversed by mistake. Once you have packed the cane, it is difficult to separate.

Join individual slices to create a field of pattern. This type of coverage is often done in the placement of individual slices instead of stacking a group of canes.

The illustrations shown reveal cross sections of the cane and how it is made into patterns. Often the cane is rotated, reversed, flipped and reduced to create the finished pattern. In viewing the illustrations, locate the original design to understand how the metamorphosis of the original design occurs.

Set 1: Create large amounts of blended clay, with colors varying in value (light to dark). Stack several sheets of the same blend together so you have thick portions to work with. Prepare (by conditioning) large portions of clay that will serve as shapes. These can be blends, spirals or bull's eyes.
• Assemble the shapes into a large cane. I would describe this as a 'hunk' of clay. The original cane is then reduced. This can be done in stages and also the form of the original design can change, for instance, into an equilateral triangle, or a right triangle.
• Following the example, the cane shape is an equilateral triangle. It first is paired, then the pairs are in a set of three, then the pairs are in a set of four. The original pairs must modify in shape to fit into 4 quarters.

• Following the example, the triangles are paired along different sides. Now the pair of right triangle shapes (forming a diamond) are bent (reshaped) into a different triangle (isosceles) before they are assembled as halves in the new pattern.
• Following the example, the diamond is bent into an isosceles triangle before it is paired, then doubled, then cubed. The square cane at the bottom reflects 16 copies of the original cane.

 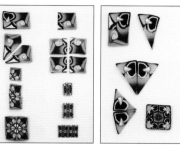

• Follow the examples
Set 1: Arrange 6 sections and reduce them. Reshape the resulting cane into a triangle.

Set 2: Alter the sections in set 2 by slicing (cropping) the original cane into a smaller unit... eliminate certain colors and shapes. Create different options in pairing. Notice the trimmed cane resembles the patterns in the whole cane (1). That's a trick with the eyes as you take a second look. They have the same essence but are in reality different.

Set 3: Slice the original cane in set 3 again to utilize a different portion of the cane. You can also reverse the pattern, instead of matching it to create rhythm.

Whole cane (1-3):
The concept behind any of the kaleidoscope processes, is that the focus is shifted if different sides are adjacent to each other.
If you had enough of a surface pattern connected, you would find all the whole cane examples included in different portions of the surface.

This wirework by Lisa Barth frames the Kaleidoscope pillow and tube beads by Barbara McGuire.

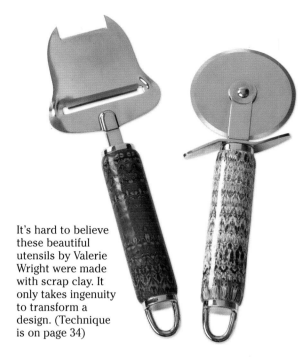

It's hard to believe these beautiful utensils by Valerie Wright were made with scrap clay. It only takes ingenuity to transform a design. (Technique is on page 34)

Just for Fun - Brain Cane

The brain cane (or ribbon cane) is a fun 'what if?' that encourages playful design. Sometimes patterns and colors do not have to 'mean' anything to be attractive. But once they are assembled, we search to give them meaning so they can be identified.

Try something different and name your own cane!

The Brain Cane: Choose attractive colors that are bright. In this example, I already knew Red, Black and White would be a classic winner.

• Assemble a double thick sheet of Red, a thin sheet of White, and an ultrathin sheet of Black to make a stack. Make sure all the sheets are well conditioned as the stack is thick to bend.

• Bend the stack back and forth like a ribbon. Smooth all cracks that may occur in the layers as you are bending.

• Don't just have ribbons. Run the full sheet along all the bends – this makes the ribbons into fingers.
• This cane does not need to be reduced to be interesting. Always estimate what diameter a cane is most effective before it is automatically reduced.

Techniques

The Evolution of a Technique

The creative process is a magnet for sharing and good times. Even the simplest discoveries can produce the 'ah ha' factor of a clever application. I experience a fulfilling bond in the sharing of ideas and the discoveries of others, which I have seen grow throughout the artistic community.

The following project is one of those delightful moments when pure play turns into ingenuity, and is refined into marvelous results.

This is a variation on the Damascus Ladder cane presented by Jody Bishel in the summer 2003 edition of Polymer Café magazine. It was presented to me by Valerie Wright who reinterpreted the information from the magazine to utilize the surface design in decorating upscale utensils (see page 33).

Val Cat Scrap Directions: Gather 6 to 8 ounces of scrap clay. Skinner blends, cane ends and canes work well. Be sure that all clay is still soft and not hard and crumbly. Randomly chop clay into small pieces.

• Gather a handful of scrap clay and form into a log, roll on the surface to smooth.
• Spread a thin layer of scrap pieces on the work surface and roll the log across the clay to pick up the pieces. Compress the log and roll on the surface to smooth. Repeat this process until all scrap clay has been added to the log. The log should resemble a squat round pop can about 3" - 4" tall.

• Hold the log in your hands and gently twist. The clay on the outside will begin to look like stripes. Continue to twist until the entire log appears striped. Be sure to twist each of the ends well.
Reshape the log into the squat pop can shape and roll on the surface to smooth. Place the log on the work surface so that the stripes are going up and down.
• Flatten the log with a roller going up and down, not side to side.
Continue to roll the log into a sheet until it is the thickness of the thickest setting on a pasta machine. It should still be 3"- 4" wide. If a pasta machine is not used, roll the log to a uniform thickness with the roller.
Place the sheet in the pasta machine on the thickest setting with the shortest end of the sheet touching the rollers. The stripes should be vertical.
Cut the rolled stripe sheet into 4" - 6" segments for easier handling.
• Place a segment of the sheet on the work surface with the stripes going side to side, not up and down. Using a stiff blade cut the ⅛" strips from the sheet. Turn each strip ¼ turn so that the cut side is up. Begin to line up each cut strip next to each other to form a new sheet.
Note: A mirror image design can be made by matching the design on each strip to the one before. Every other strip will need to be flipped to form the mirror image. Once the strips are formed into a sheet, gently roll the sheet with a roller to smooth the surface and adhere the strips to each other. This sheet can also be put through the pasta machine at progressively thinner settings until the desired thickness is obtained.
Use the sheet to cover an item or use in jewelry. Before baking, apply a thin layer of liquid clay to the clay to minimize lines between the strips.

Applique canes create patterns of scenes.

Projects with Canes

What do you do with a cane after you've made it? Usually it is thinly sliced and the slices are rolled or pressed into another body of clay. This can be a clay bead, or a sheet of clay, or you can use cane slices as beads themselves.

The following projects are meant to be examples of ways that you can enhance designs with cane work.

Tips for Finishing

Design elements and principles are key – remember the form of an object is a gratifying challenge.

Texture is an added option. Use it. A smooth texture is also a texture. A glossy texture is a texture. Note: For high shine, sand the finished piece with 400 & 600 WET sandpaper (using water and a drop of soap as you sand) for a smooth finish. Buff this finish with a muslin wheel for a glossy shine.

Less is more. Negative space is important.

Pattern is fun, repetition creates rhythm. These are found in nature and are pleasing to the eye and soul.

Be consistent. Similar designs go together. Add contrast for effect, not confusion or competition.

Finish the item well. Use bead caps, edges and findings to add finesse to a finished piece.

A Rolled Bead: The key to a bead is its shape. Roll a ball of clay and cover it with some portions of shaded color. I like to use cutters to cut out scrap from shaded sheets and apply the sheets to the bead.
Attach slices of the cane in random patterns and roll the shape smooth.

Trim excess clay where slices overlap.
Bake the clay as the manufacturer suggests and drill a hole through the bead after it has baked.